I0020157

Adobe Photoshop 2023 Handbook

The Step by Step Photoshop Manual
with Illustrations for Beginners

By

Jonjo Penney

Table of Contents

Chapter 1: Getting to Know the Work Area

Starting to Work in Adobe Photoshop

To quickly access tools and options for editing and adding elements to your picture, the Adobe Photoshop work area has menus, toolbars, and panels. Installing plug-ins, which are pieces of third-party software, is another way to add functionality.

In Photoshop, bitmapped digital images consisting of continuous-tone pictures divided into a collection of tiny squares or image components are the most common type of file. You can also use vector graphics, which are illustrations with slick lines that maintain their clarity at any size. In addition, Photoshop allows you to produce original art as well as import pictures from a variety of sources, including:

- Pictures were taken with a digital camera or a smartphone.

- Stock photos, like those from the Adobe Stock service.

- Images from documents, transparencies, negatives, graphics, or photos.

- Work produced by sketching or painting software.

Starting Photoshop

You will launch Adobe Photoshop and reset the default preferences to commence:

1. To restore the default settings, click the Adobe Photoshop 2023 icon in your Start menu (Windows), Launchpad, or Dock (Mac). At the same time, hold down Ctrl+Alt+Shift (Windows) or Command+Option+Shift (MacOS).

   If Adobe Photoshop 2023 isn't displayed, enter Photoshop into the search field in the taskbar (Windows) or Spotlight (Mac OS) and hit Enter or Return when the Adobe Photoshop 2023 program icon appears.

2. Click Yes to confirm that you want to remove the Adobe Photoshop Settings file when asked.

Using the Home screen

The Home screen, which offers you several ways to start, is the first item you see after opening Photoshop:

There is a list of view choices on the left:

- **Home**: Home offers a tour and assists you in using and learning about the current edition. A Recent section of previously opened documents will show up at the foot of the Home screen once you've accessed at least one locally stored document.

- **Learn:** This provides links to tutorials that launch in Photoshop and walk you through the stages of a lesson while you use Photoshop itself.

- **Your files:** Photoshop Cloud Documents, including those you made on gadgets like an iPad, are listed under Your Files.

- **Shared with You:** Using the File > Invite command, you can see a list of Cloud Documents others have asked you to view.

- **Lightroom Photos:** Images linked to your Creative Cloud account are listed in Lightroom Photos, an online photo storage service (not Lightroom Classic local storage).

- **Deleted:** If you change your mind and decide to retrieve the Cloud Documents you've deleted, they are listed in the Deleted list (similar to the Recycle Bin or Trash on your computer desktop). Only Cloud Documents are included in this inventory; any files you deleted from your computer's local storage or Lightroom Photos are not included.

How to open a document

There are numerous methods to open documents in Photoshop. However, you will employ the conventional Open command here, which functions similarly to other applications you have undoubtedly used the Open command in.

1. Select File > Upload. If a dialog window with the heading Cloud Documents appears, select On Your Computer from the list of options there.

2. Navigate to the peachpit.com website's folder that you copied to your hard disk.

3. Click View after selecting the file. If the Embedded Profile Mismatch dialog box opens, click OK; otherwise, click No when prompted to update the text layers.

   In the usual Photoshop workspace, the good file opens in a separate window. The book's final files provide an overview of the output from each endeavor.

4. Select File > Close, or select the document window's tab's close button (the x next to the filename). Keep Photoshop open, and don't save any modifications to the file. The filename is added to the Home screen's Recent section.

Using the tools

Photoshop offers a comprehensive collection of tools for creating complex graphics for use on the web, in print, and on mobile devices. Although the wealth of Photoshop tools and tool configurations could easily fill the complete book, the aim of this guide is different. Instead, using a few key tools on a practice project will help you acquire experience. You will learn more tools and techniques in each session. After completing all the classes in this book, you'll be well-equipped to explore other aspects of Photoshop.

How to select and use a tool from the tools panel

The tall, narrow panel to the left of the work area's center is the Tools panel. It includes viewing tools, foreground- and background-color selection boxes, drawing and editing tools, and selection tools for colors.

1. To access the 01Start.psd file, select File > Open, go to the folder, and double-click it.

2. To switch to a double-column layout, which may be more beneficial for smaller displays like those on laptops, click the double arrows directly above the Tools panel. To return to a single-column Tools panel, which may better use the room on a large desktop display, click the double arrows again.

3. Look at the status indicator at the bottom of the document window (Mac OS) or work area (Windows), and pay attention to the percentage displayed on the far left. It displays the image's zoom degree or current enlargement view.

4. When a tooltip shows, move the pointer over the magnifying glass icon in the Tools panel. For example, the computer shortcut and tool name (Zoom tool) are displayed in the tooltip (Z).

5. To pick the Zoom tool, click its icon in the Tools panel.

6. The text window with the pointer. Now the pointer resembles a tiny magnifying glass with a plus symbol in the middle (Zoom tool when increasing magnification).

7. Anywhere in the document window can be clicked.

8. Click anywhere in the picture while holding down the Alt or Option keys to make the Zoom tool pointer appear with a minus sign in the center of the magnifying glass (Zoom tool when decreasing magnification). Release the Shift or Option key after that.

   Drag the Zoom tool to the right after clicking anywhere on the picture if Scrubby Zoom is checked in the options bar. The picture gets bigger. To expand out, move the Zoom tool to the left.

9. If Scrubby Zoom is already chosen, deselect it in the options bar. Then, drag a rectangle to encompass the rose blossom using the Zoom tool partially.

10. The area you outlined in your rectangle now fills the full document window as the image enlarges.

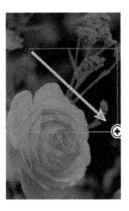

11. To view the full image once more, select Fit Screen from the options bar to view the full image.

How to sample a color

When you paint on a layer in Photoshop, it employs foreground and background colors. The foreground hue, such as the color loaded for a brush, is what you'll typically focus on. Black and white are the usual foreground and background colors, respectively. There are several methods to alter the foreground and background colors. One method is to sample a hue from the image using the Eyedropper tool. For example, to replicate the blue of one ribbon when creating a different one, you'll use the Eyedropper tool to capture the color.

1. The Ribbons layer will be displayed first to see the hue you want to sample. Select the Visibility column in the Layers panel to make the Ribbons layer visible. An eye icon (Eye icon controlling layer visibility) shows in that column when a layer is visible.

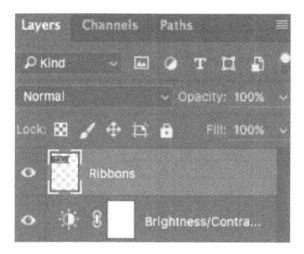

2. The document window displays a ribbon with the words "Happy Birthday" inscribed.

3. Make the Ribbons layer the active component in the Layers panel by selecting it.

4. In the Tools tab, choose the Eyedropper tool (Eyedropper tool).

5. Click the Happy Birthday ribbon's blue portion to view a blue hue sample.

Working with tools and tool properties

In the previous activity, when you chose the Zoom tool, you could change the view of the currently open document window using the options bar. You'll discover more about configuring tool settings with panels, panel menus, options bars, and context menus. You'll employ all these techniques as you work with tools to attach the second ribbon to your greeting card.

How to set the unit of measure

In Photoshop, you can modify the standard of measurement you employ. For example, work in inches since this greeting card will be produced.

1. Select Photoshop > Options > Units & Rulers (Windows) or Edit > Preferences > Units & Rulers (Mac) from the menu (macOS).

2. Select Inches from the Rulers menu in the Units section, then press OK.

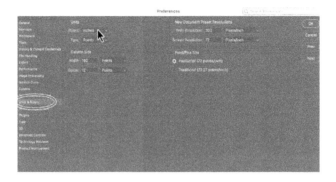

How to use context menus

A context menu appears beneath the pointer instead of the options from a menu bar. It includes options and instructions relevant to the object under the pointer and the current selection or document state. A context menu can save time by displaying pertinent commands where the pointer is, so you don't have to search the menu bar. Typically, the commands on a context menu are also available in the menu bar or panel menus. Right-click or shortcut windows are other names for context menus.

1. If necessary, adjust the perspective (zoom or scroll) to make the bottom third of the card visible.

2. In the Tools tab, choose the Rectangular Marquee tool (Rectangular Marquee tool).

3. Draw a selection with the Rectangular Marquee tool that is 0.75 inches tall by 2.5 inches wide and ends at the right border of the card. Photoshop shows the width and height of the selected region as you move the tool.

4. In the Tools tab, choose the Brush tool (Brush tool).

5. To access the context menu for the Brush tool in the document window, right-click (Windows) or control-click (Mac) anywhere in the picture.

6. Expand the General Brushes preset group (folder) by clicking the arrow next to it, choose the first brush (Soft Round), and fix the size to 65 pixels.

7. To dismiss the context menu, key in either Enter or Return.

8. Ensure that the Ribbons layer is still selected in the Layers window, and then use the Brush tool to paint the entire selected area blue. You can't paint outside the selection, so don't worry about remaining inside.

9. Select > Deselect should be used to remove all selections once the bar has been filled in.

How to select and use a hidden tool

One tool is displayed for each set of tools in the Tools panel to conserve screen real estate. Behind that instrument are the other tools in the group. You can tell that other tools are accessi toble but tucked away under a button by the tiny triangle in the lower-right corner of the button.

You will use the Polygonal Lasso tool to eliminate a triangular cut to make the color bar match the ribbon at the top of the card.

1. Place the cursor over the third tool from the top in the Tools panel to display the tooltip. The keyboard shortcut L for the Lasso tool is listed in the utility tip.

2. Use one of the following techniques to access the Polygonal Lasso tool, which is concealed behind the Lasso tool:

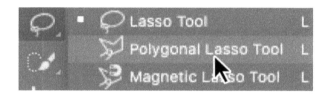

- Select the Polygonal Lasso tool from the pop-up selection of hidden tools by pressing and holding the mouse button over the Lasso tool.

- To cycle through the hidden tools until the Polygonal Lasso tool is chosen, Alt-click the tool button in the Tools panel on Windows or Option-click the tool button on Mac OS.

- Press Shift+L to switch between the group's utilities (the Lasso, Polygonal Lasso, and Magnetic Lasso tools).

3. Place the pointer over the freshly painted blue bar's left border. To begin your pick, click to the left of the bar's

upper-left corner. Just outside the colored area is where you should start your pick.

4. Click roughly midway between the top and bottom of the bar after adjusting the cursor to the right by a little more than a quarter of an inch. You are forming the triangle's bottom half. It doesn't have to be flawless.

5. To make the second half of the triangle, click just to the left of the bottom-left corner of the bar.

6. To complete the triangle, click your starting spot.

7. To make a notch for your ribbon, press the Delete key on your computer to remove the chosen portion of the colored bar.

8. Pick Chose > To remove the region you deleted, click Deselect.

How to undo actions in Photoshop

You would always make a good decision in an ideal society. Never would you select the incorrect item. You could always foresee precisely how certain actions would bring your design ideas to life as you had imagined. Never would you have to go back.

Photoshop provides you the ability to go back and undo actions so that you can try different things in the real world. In addition, knowing you can stop the procedure allows you to experiment without restriction.

Even novice computer users rapidly learn to value the well-known Undo command. First, you'll use it to take a step backward, followed by another movement backward. Here, you'll return to the light shade you initially selected for the name.

1. To undo your previous move, select Edit > Undo Edit Type Layer or press Ctrl+Z (Windows) or Command+Z (macOS). The name changes back to its original hue.

2. To reapply the orange hue to the name, select Edit > Redo Edit Type Layer or press Ctrl+Shift+Z (Windows) or Command+Shift+Z (macOS).

3. The Undo command (or its keyboard shortcut) allows you to retrace one step at a time, so if you want to undo five steps, you can use it five times. The Redo instruction operates similarly.

4. Use the Move tool (Move tool) to drag the name to the center of the blue bar once the name has returned to the desired hue.

5. Save the file.

Chapter 2: Basic Photo Corrections

Resolution and image size

Ensure the Image has the right number of pixels when editing it in Photoshop for a particular purpose. Pixels are tiny squares that define an image and determine its level of detail. The number of pixels along the width and height of an image, or its pixel dimensions, can be used to calculate this.

The number of pixels in an image can be calculated by dividing the breadth by the height in pixels. As an illustration, a picture with 1000 x 1000 pixels has 1,000,000 pixels (or one megapixel), while an image with 2000 x 2000 pixels has 4,000,000 pixels (four megapixels). Therefore, file size and upload/download times are influenced by pixel measurements.

Resolution in Photoshop refers to the number of pixels per physical measurements, such as pixels per inch (ppi).

Does altering the resolution change how much space a file takes up? Only if the size of the pixels changes. For instance, a 7 x 7 inch image at 300 ppi has a pixel size of 2100 x 2100; if the size in inches or the ppi number (resolution) is changed while the pixel size remains the same, the file size does not change. However, if you alter the size in inches without altering the ppi number (or vice versa), the file size and pixel dimensions will change. For example, the pixel size must change to 504 504 pixels if the picture in the previous example is changed to 72 ppi while keeping its original size of 7 7 inches, and the file size reduces correspondingly.

Depending on the desired output, different resolution requirements apply. For example, when an image's ppi number is less than or equal to 150 to 200 ppi, it may be deemed to have low resolution. However, because it can benefit from the device resolution provided by professional or fine-art printers and high-resolution (Retina/HiDPI) device displays, an image with a ppi number above 200 ppi is typically regarded as having high resolution.

The resolution that our eyes truly perceive depends on variables like viewing distance and output technology, which also impacts resolution requirements. For example, a 220-ppi laptop monitor may have the same high resolution as a 360-ppi smartphone display due to distance. However, a high-end printing press or fine-art inkjet printer, which may reproduce at 300 ppi or more, might need more sharpness at 220 ppi. At the same time, a billboard on a highway can display a 50 ppi picture that is perfectly sharp due to the distance (hundreds of feet).

Your pictures may not necessarily match the device resolution of high-resolution printers because of how display and output technologies function. For instance, even though some photo-quality inkjet printers and commercial printing platesetters have device resolutions of 2400 dots per inch (dpi) or higher, the ideal image resolution to transmit to those devices may only be 200 to 360 ppi for photos. This is so that tones and hues can be created using the device dots, which are organized into larger halftone cells or inkjet dot patterns. Similarly, images may only sometimes need to be 500 pixels per inch for a smartphone monitor. Again, ask your production team or output service provider to confirm the pixel sizes or ppi value they demand in the final images you give, regardless of the medium.

How to Open a File With Adobe Bridge

You can either work from the initial start files and then download them from the peachpit.com website again if you want a fresh start, or you can make copies of these files and save them under different names or locations.

In Adobe Bridge, a visual file browser that makes locating the image file you need easier, you will begin by comparing the original scan to the final Image.

1. To restore the original settings, simultaneously open Photoshop and press Ctrl+Alt+Shift (Windows) or Command+Option+Shift (macOS).

2. Click Yes to confirm that you want to remove the Adobe Photoshop Settings file when asked.

3. Select "File"> "Explore In Bridge." If Bridge asks you if you want to activate the Photoshop extension, choose Yes or OK.

4. To make the lessons in the Lessons folder shown in the Content panel, click the Folders tab in the top-left corner and then navigate to the folder you downloaded onto your hard drive, Lessons.

5. Choose File> Add To Favorites while the Lessons folder is still chosen in the Folders panel.

6. To access the panel, select the Favorites tab and the Lessons folder. Then, double-click the folder in the Content tab.

7. Drag the thumbnail slider to the right at the bottom of the Bridge window to expand the thumbnails in the Content panel.

    Be aware of the Image's crookedness, comparatively dull colors, green color cast, and distracting crease in the 02Start.tif File.

8. To view the 02Start.tif File in Photoshop, double-click the thumbnail. If the Embedded Profile Mismatch dialog window appears, click OK.

9. Select Download > Save As in Photoshop. Create a file named 02Working.psd and select Photoshop from the Format option. Next, select Save.

How to straighten and crop the Image in Photoshop

The Crop tool will be used to resize, crop, and align the picture. Cropped particles are typically deleted after cropping.

1. Choose the Crop tool from the Tools menu (Crop tool).

   To help you concentrate on the cropped area, crop handles show, and a crop shield covers the space outside the cropping region.

2. Select W, H, or Resolution in the options bar. Select A Preset Aspect Ratio or Crop Size selection. (The default number is a ratio.) There is a crop enhancement.

3. Enter 7 in for the width, 7 in for the height, and 200 px/in for the resolution in the options box.

4. In the options menu, select the Straighten icon. The Straighten tool now has the cursor.

5. To draw a straight line across the top edge, click the top-left corner of the picture (where the sky ends), hold down the mouse button while doing so, and then let go.

   The line you drew will be parallel to the top of the image region after Photoshop straightens the Image. So, for example, you drew a line across the top of the picture, but you could also draw it along any precisely vertical or horizontal part of the picture.

6. To remove the white border, move lp p p the crop rectangle's sides inward. Place the pointer inside the crop rectangle and drag the Image if you need to change the picture's position inside the crop.

7. To approve the crop, press Enter or Return.

8. Click the arrow in the status area at the bottom of the program window, and then select Document Dimensions from the pop-up menu that appears if the picture dimensions are not already visible there.

9. The Save option is found under Edit > Save. If the Photoshop Format Options dialog window appears, click OK.

How to adjust the color and tone

To eliminate the color cast and modify the Image's color and tone, use the Curves and Levels editing layers. Although the Curves or Levels choices may appear difficult, have confidence.

1. Select the Curves icon from the Adjustments window (first row, third button). The Curves adjustment layer is added, and the Properties panel's settings appear for it.

2. Pick the White Point tool from the Properties panel's left side.

What white value should be turned a neutral white is determined by the White Point tool. All other colors and tones change per the definition. It is a quick method to remove a color cast and adjust image brightness when done properly. The brightest neutral area of the Image that includes detail should be selected as the white point, not a blown-out area like the sun or a lamp or a specular highlight like the sun's reflection on chrome. All other hues and tones change per the definition. It is a quick method to remove a color cast and adjust image brightness when done properly. The brightest neutral area of the Image that includes detail should be selected as the white point, not a blown-out area like the sun or a lamp or a specular highlight like the sun's reflection on chrome.

3. Select a white stripe on the girl's dress.

Using the White Point tool to click on the white stripe, you can improve the picture by changing the brightness and color balance based on how far the sampled color is from neutral white. For example, a stripe on the woman's dress, the child's sailor dress, or other white regions can all be clicked. By clicking the area closest to neutral bright white in the actual world, you'll usually get the most even result.

To improve the Image's tonal spectrum, use a Levels adjustment layer.

4. Click the Levels icon (Levels Icon Adjustment Panel) (first row, second button) to create a Levels adjustment layer in the Adjustments panel (if necessary, click its tab to make it visible).

The Properties tab shows a histogram for both Curves and Levels, which is a graph showing the distribution of tonal values in the Image from black on the left to white on the right. In terms of levels, the black point (the tonal level you want to set as the darkest in the Image) is represented by the left triangle under the histogram, the white point (the tonal level you want to set as the lightest in the Image) is represented by the right triangle, and the midtones are represented by the middle triangle.

5. Drag the left triangle (black spot) under the histogram to the right; significant shadow tones can be seen. We valued it at 15. Below 15, all tones turn dark.

6. To change the midtones, slightly drag the center triangle to the right. We scored a.90.

To make the Image simpler to work with while you make adjustments, flatten it now. When a picture is flattened, all of its layers are combined into the Background layer. Only flatten if you no longer require the ability to modify the changes you previously made using different layers.

7. Select Flatten Picture under Layer.

The Background layer and the Adjustment levels combine.

How to Use the Spot Healing Brush tool

The photo's steam needs to be removed next. To remove the seam, utilize the Spot Healing Brush. You'll use it to handle a few other problems while you're at it.

Blemishes and other flaws are swiftly eliminated by the Spot Healing Brush tool. It takes a sample of the pixels in the vicinity of the retouched region and compares their texture, lighting, transparency, and shading to the pixels that are being corrected.

The Spot Healing Brush performs well whenever a uniform appearance is close to the areas you want to retouch. It is particularly good at removing imperfections from portraits.

1. To see the crease, zoom in.

2. From the Tools panel, choose the Spot Healing Brush too

3. Open the Brush pop-up panel in the options menu, choose a brush with a Size of approximately 25 px and 100% Hardness, and ensure Content-Aware is checked.

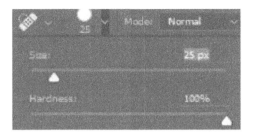

4. Place the Spot Healing Brush at the top of the crease in the document window and move it down the crease. It's acceptable if repairing the crease requires some smaller passes. The stroke initially looks black as you drag, but when you let go of the mouse, the painted region is "healed."

5. In the upper-right corner of the picture, zoom in to see the white hair. Then cover the hair with the Spot Restorative Brush.

6. To see the entire sky, enlarge the Image if required. Then, select the Spot Healing Brush wherever you want to remove any undesirable spots.

7. Save your current work.

How to apply a content-aware patch

Use the Patch tool to eliminate more noticeable undesirable elements, like a stranger near the photo's right border. The Patch tool blends with the surrounding content almost seamlessly in Content-Aware mode.

1. Hover the Object Selection tool (Object Selection tool) over each individual in the Image without clicking in the Tools panel. When hovered, each individual is highlighted.

   By clicking a highlighted area, the item is selected after being automatically detected by the Object Selection tool. But the selection will be lacking if the highlight doesn't cover the full subject. So it would help if you dragged the tool into, helping guarantee a more thorough selection.

2. After moving the child with the Object Selection tool, let go of the mouse. The final choice is appropriate for both the full child and his shadow.

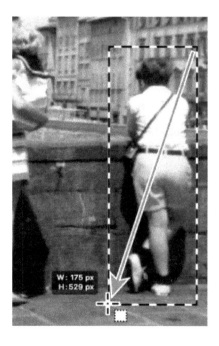

3. Enter 2 for Pixels, select Select > Modify > Expand, and press OK.

4. Select the Patch tool (patch symbol) tucked away beneath the Spot Healing Brush tool in the Tools panel (Spot Healing Brush tool). Select Content-Aware from the Patch menu in the options window. In the Structure box, enter 4.

5. Place the pointer inside the selection and drag it to the left to omit the lady and kid and replace the boy with the wall and background. When the patch looks satisfactory, click and drag the mouse to release it.

6. Choose Select > Deselect.

Although not quite perfect, the result is still impressive.

How to repair areas with the Clone Stamp tool

With the Clone Stamp tool, you can swap out pixels in one region of an image for those in another. This tool can remove obtrusive items from your photos and fill in blank spaces in pictures you scan from imperfect originals.

To improve the patch edge lineup, you'll use the Clone Stamp tool to smooth out differences in the height of the bridge wall and the building's windows.

1. Select a 60-px brush with a 30% Hardness by choosing the Clone Stamp tool (Clone Stamp tool icon) in the Tools window. Verify that the Aligned choice is chosen.

2. Select a spot where the top of the bridge wall is flat and move the Clone Stamp tool there. To smooth out the patched area, you should duplicate that region.

3. Click with the Alt or Option keys on a Windows or Mac computer to sample that spot as a starting point. (The pointer becomes target crosshairs when you select Alt or Option.)

4. Release the mouse button after dragging the Clone Stamp tool across the bridge wall's top to even out the patched region.

5. Drag the Clone Stamp tool across the bridge wall's bottom where you patched it from a source spot where the wall's bottom is even.

6. Deselect Aligned and choose a smaller brush size. Then, choose a source point over the bottom row of windows on the right of the structure you patched. There, click to make precise frames.

7. Repeat step 6 to change the building's lowest point and the wall in front of it if necessary. Be sure to retouch any areas that the cloning has caused to duplicate.

8. You can choose to use a smaller brush size to add finishing touches to the stones in the patched-up area of the wall.

9. Save your work.

How to Sharpen the Image

Sharpening the picture should be your final step in photo retouching. The Smart Sharpen filter in Photoshop offers the most power over the various sharpening options available. You'll get rid of any blemishes first because sharpening might highlight them.

1. For a good view of the boy's shirt, zoom in by about 400%. The colored spots you can see are scan-related artifacts.

2. Select Filter > Noise > Dust & Scratches.

3. Leave the Radius and Threshold values in the Dust & Scratches dialog window at 1 pixel and 0, respectively, and click OK to accept the default settings.

4. Select Filter > Sharpen > Smart Sharpen.

5. Make sure Preview is selected in the Smart Sharpen dialog box so you can examine the results of any settings you change in the document window.

   To view different portions of the Image, drag inside the dialog box's preview window. You can zoom in and out using the magnification buttons below the thumbnail.

6. Make sure the Delete menu's Lens Blur option is selected.

   In the Smart Sharpen dialog window, you can select to delete Lens Blur, Gaussian Blur, or Motion Blur. Lens Blur offers reduced sharpening halos and finer precision sharpening. Gaussian Blur improves contrast in an image's borders. Motion Blur minimizes the impacts of blur brought on by the camera or subject movement during the photo-taking process.

7. To sharpen the picture, move the Amount slider to about 60%.

8. Aim for 1.5 on the Radius parameter.

    The Radius value establishes how many pixels beyond the border pixels impact sharpening. Typically, the Radius option should be increased as the resolution increases.

9. Click OK to use the Smart Sharpen filter once you're happy with the outcomes.

10. Choose File> Save, and then close the project file.

Chapter 3: Working with Selections

Selecting and selection tools

A two-step procedure is used to edit a pixel layer's pixels in a specific region. To start, use one of the selection tools to select (mark) the area you want to alter. After that, implement a filter or another feature, such as moving the selected pixels to a new location, to make the desired changes. Changes you make when a selection is active only impact the area you have chosen; they have no effect elsewhere.

Utilizing the finest selection tools depends on two things: the kind of selection you're looking for and the visual traits that set an area apart, like shape, color, or content. The Tools panel groups similar picking tools:

- **Content-and edge-based selections:** The Object Selection tool (Object Selection tool) uses machine learning to identify subjects that you select with a simple click or drag; this is a quick and easy way to select people, animals, and other non-geometric shapes. The Quick Selection tool (Quick Selection tool) quickly "paints" a selection by looking for distinct content regions in the image.

- **Color-based selections:** The Magic Wand tool (Magic Wand tool) selects parts of an image based on similarity in pixel color. It's useful for selecting odd-shaped areas with a specific range of colors or tones.

- **Geometric selections:** The Rectangular Marquee tool (Rectangular Marquee tool) selects a rectangular area. The Elliptical Marquee tool (Elliptical Marquee tool) selects an elliptical area. The Single Row Marquee tool (Single Row Marquee tool) and Single Column Marquee tool (Single Column Marquee tool) select either a 1-pixel-high row or a 1-pixel-wide column, respectively.

- **Freehand selections:** The Lasso tool (Lasso tool) traces a freehand selection around an area. The Polygonal Lasso tool (Polygonal Lasso tool) lays down straight-line segments around an area. The Magnetic Lasso tool (Magnetic Lasso tool) automatically follows edges, typically giving the best results when high contrast exists between the area you want to select and its surroundings.

Getting started

As you explore the selection tools in Photoshop, you'll first look at the picture you'll produce.

- Start Photoshop and press Ctrl+Alt+Shift (Windows) or Command+Option+Shift (Mac) at the same time to return to the preset settings.

- Click Yes to confirm that you want to remove the Adobe Photoshop Settings file when asked.

- To launch Adobe Bridge, select File > Browse In Bridge.

- Click the Lessons folder in the Favorites menu. Then, to view its data, double-click the folder in the Content panel.

- Examine the 03End.psd document. If you want to see the picture more detail, slide the thumbnail to the right.

- A piece of coral, a sand dollar, a mussel, a nautilus, and a plate of tiny shells are all included in the shadow box craft. Arranging these components, which were scanned collectively onto the single page you see in the 03Start.psd file, is the task for this session.

How to Use cloud documents

Photoshop documents can grow in size, particularly when high-resolution pictures have numerous layers. Large file sizes upload and download more slowly when working with documents saved online; if you have a limited data plan, you may quickly use your allotted data. Adobe cloud documents use file formats optimized for networks to help you modify online documents effectively.

It's simple to use cloud documents; you only have to save them to cloud documents. Your Photoshop document will now be displayed in the cloud documents section of the Photoshop Home screen and have the filename extension ".psdc" to indicate that it is a cloud document due to what you just did. You don't need to consider it because converting to the PSDC format is automated.

1. To view the image file in Photoshop, double-click the 03Start.psd thumbnail in Bridge. The document was viewed from your local storage.

2. Select Save to Creative Cloud under Project > Save As. Click the Save To Cloud Documents button first if the typical Save As dialog window appears.

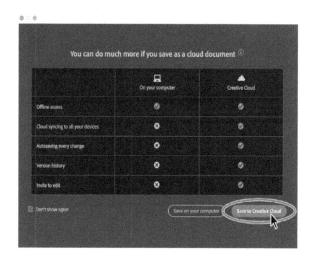

3. Click Save after renaming the file to 03WorkingCloud. The document is put on Cloud Documents.

You can see a cloud icon in the document window tab before the filename, and the filename now terminates in. psdc.

4. Close the document.

How to Use the Magic Wand tool

The Magic Wand tool chooses pixels that fall within a certain hue or range of colors. Therefore, it works best when the area you want to pick has a tone or color that stands out from the surrounding area.

The Magic Wand tool's variety of tonal levels, beginning with the pixel you click, is determined by the Tolerance option. The color you click, along with 32 lighter and 32 darker tones of that color, is selected by the default tolerance number of 32. Try increasing the Tolerance value if the Magic Wand tool doesn't pick the entire area as expected. Reduce the Tolerance amount if the tool makes an excessive number of selections.

1. You can zoom in to see the full sand dollar in detail by choosing the Zoom tool from the Tools panel.

2. Choose the Magic Wand tool tucked away beneath the Object Picking tool (Object Selection tool).

3. Verify that the Tolerance number is 32 in the options bar. This value determines the wand's hue selection range.

4. On the crimson background outside the sand dollar, select the Magic Wand tool.

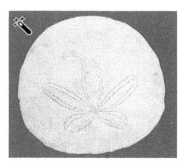

Due to the fact that every color in the background is sufficiently similar to the pixel you clicked, the Magic Wand tool precisely selected the red background (within the 32 levels specified in the Tolerance setting). But let's start over because that's the body we want.

5. Pick Select > Deselect.

6. Click while moving the Magic Wand tool over the sand dollar.

    Examine the animated selection marquee that pops up over the sand dollar attentively. If this was the ideal choice, the choice marquee would closely resemble the sand dollar's outer border. However, note that some of sand dollar's interior spaces have selection marquees because their colors are more than 32 levels different from the color you selected (the Tolerance setting). Because it excludes all interior colors, the present option could be more effective.

    Increasing the Tolerance value can frequently help you choose a topic with the same color and value against a relatively plain background. However, a wide Tolerance value is more likely to pick undesirable portions of the background the more complex the topic or background. A distinct selection tool, like the Quick Selection tool, is typically preferable in that scenario. You'll do that next, but let's remove the currently selected option first.

7. Choose Select > Deselect.

How to Use the Quick Selection tool

Click or drag the Quick Selection tool inside a topic to have it search for the subject's edges. You can add or remove selection areas until you have precisely the area you want. The Quick Selection tool, which is more aware of picture content than the Magic Wand tool, which only relies on color similarity, performs better in this situation. Let's see if the Quick Selection feature selects the sand dollar more accurately.

- In the Tools tab, choose the Quick Selection tool (Quick Selection tool). It is paired with both the Magic Wand tool and the Object Selection tool (Magic Wand tool).

- The choice Enhance Edge should be selected.

By choosing Enhance Edge, you should get a better selection with edges that are more accurate to the item. You might experience a small delay when using Enhance Edge if your computer is older or slower.

- Drag or click inside the sand dollar (do not cross over into the background).

The Quick Selection tool locates the complete edge automatically by examining what content is likely related to the area where you clicked or dragged, selecting the entire sand dollar. The Quick Selection tool can quickly isolate the sand dollar because it is a simple object. Click or drag over the areas you want to include in the selection when the Quick Selection tool doesn't originally finish it.

How to move a selected area

Any modifications you make after selecting only affect the pixels in the selection. These modifications have no impact on the remainder of the picture.

You can use the Move tool to move the selected region to another area of the composition. The pixels you shift will replace those below them because there is only one layer in this image. You can try various locations for the selection you're moving before you commit it because this change is temporary until you deselect the moved pixels.

1. Repeat the prior exercise to select the sand dollar if it still needs to be selected.

2. To make the shadow box and the sand dollar visible, zoom out.

3. Choosing the Shift tool (Move tool). The sand dollar is still the selection, as you can see.

4. Drag the chosen region (the sand dollar) to the "A"-designated area in the frame's top left corner. Place it

over the silhouette in the frame, casting a shade over the lower-left portion of it.

5. Click Select > Deselect, followed by File > Save, are the options.

Deselecting an option can be done in several different ways. Choose Select > Deselect, hit Ctrl+D (Windows) or Command+D (Mac OS), or use any selection tool to click outside the selection.

How to Use the Object Selection tool

All you need to do to use the Object Selection tool is make a rough selection around the item you want to select, and the tool will recognize the object and make a precise selection just for it. The Object Selection tool will typically be much quicker than attempting to draw that erratic outline by hand for an object with a complex outline, like the coral.

Select the Magic Wand tool (Magic Wand tool), which is paired with the Quick Selection tool (Quick Selection tool), and the Object Selection tool (Object Selection tool) (Magic Wand tool).

Draw a pick around the coral chunk. It's optional for it to be exact or focused. It's crucial that the selection is constrained, leaving little room between the coral and the selection marquee's borders. Simply displaying the item you want to select in Photoshop.

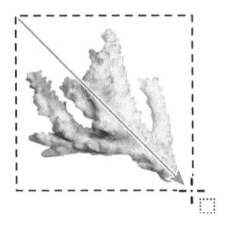

By dragging the coral to the region of the shadow box marked "B" with the Move tool selected, you can position it so that a shadow is cast to the coral's left and below.

After selecting Pick > Deselect, save your work.

How to Select the lasso tool

As we previously stated, the Lasso tool, the Polygonal Lasso tool, and the Magnetic Lasso tool are the three lasso tools available in Photoshop. Using keyboard shortcuts, you can switch between the Lasso and the Polygonal Lasso tools to create selections that call for freehand and straight lines. For example, to choose the bivalve, use the Lasso tool. Alternating between straight-line and freehand selections takes some experience; if you select the mussel incorrectly, deselect it and try again.

1. Select the Zoom tool (Zoom tool) and hit the mussel to zoom in to at least 100% if the window's magnification is less than that.

2. Choose the Lasso tool (Lasso tool). Drag around the mussel's rounded end, starting at the lower-left corner and tracing the outline as precisely as possible. Never let go of the mouse handle.

3. Press the Alt (Windows) or Option (MacOS) key and then let go of the mouse button to transform the lasso pointer to a polygonal shape as you approach a corner or straight section of the edge (Polygonal Lasso tool). Keep holding down the Shift or Option key.

4. Place anchor points by clicking along the mussel's end as you trace its contours. Throughout this procedure, keep holding down the Shift or Option key. It enables you to cut out segments along the selection that are precisely straight.

5. When you reach the tip of the mussel, hold down the mouse button as you release the Alt or Option key. The pointer again appears as the lasso icon.

6. Carefully drag around the tip of the mussel, holding down the mouse button.

7. When you've finished tracing the tip and have reached the straight sections along the mussel's lower side, click Alt or Option once more before letting go of the mouse button. As necessary, click along the straight sections of the mussel's bottom side. Trace the mussel's edges, straight and curved, until you return to the left end, where your pick began.

8. After clicking the selection's starting position, release Alt or Option. Now the bivalve has been completely chosen. Keep the mussel chosen for the following activity.

How to Rotate a selection

1. Verify that the mussel is still chosen before you start.

2. To resize the document window to suit your screen, select View > Fit On Screen.

   Drag the chosen mussel to the "D" area of the shadow box while holding down the Ctrl (Windows) or Command (MacOS) key.

3. Select Edit > Transform > Rotate.

4. Step outside the bounding area to transform the pointer into a curved, two-headed arrow (Pointer icon indicating that dragging rotates selected pixels). The bivalve must be rotated 90 degrees by dragging. You can check the angle in the Rotate box in the options bar or in the transformation numbers shown next to the pointer. To complete the change, press Enter or Return.

5. If required, choose the Move tool and drag to reposition the mussel while leaving a shadow that blends in with the others. Pick > Deselect when you're finished.

6. Choose File > Save.

How to Select the Magnetic Lasso tools

Edges with strong contrast can be manually selected with the Magnetic Lasso tool. The selection border instantly snaps to the edge between regions of contrast when you use the Magnetic Lasso tool to draw. You can also control the selection path by periodically clicking the mouse to add anchor points to the selection border.

Use the Magnetic Lasso tool to pick the nautilus and move it to the shadow box.

1. Choose the Zoom tool (Zoom tool), then click the nautilus to at least 100% of the magnification level.

2. Choose the Magnetic Lasso tool, which is tucked beneath the Lasso tool (Lasso tool).

3. To trace the outline of the nautilus, click once along its left border and then move the Magnetic Lasso tool along the edge.

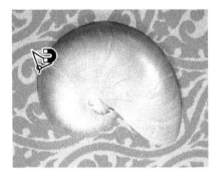

The tool instantly adds fastening points and snaps to the edge of the nautilus even if you are not holding down the mouse button.

4. When you return to the nautilus's left side, double-click to close the selection and bring the Magnetic Lasso tool

back to its beginning position. The Magnetic Lasso tool can be moved over the starting spot and clicked once.

5. Double-click the Hand tool (Hand tool) to fill the full window.

6.

7. Drag the nautilus onto its silhouette in the area of the frame marked "E" using the Move tool, leaving a shade below it and to the left of it.

8. Pick > Deselect, followed by File > Save, are the options.

Selecting from a center point

In some circumstances, drawing a selection from an object's center point makes it simpler to create elliptical or rectangular selections. This method will choose the screw head for the shadow box sides.

1. By choosing the Zoom tool (Zoom tool), you can magnify the bolt by about 300%. Ensure that your document window can see the complete screw head.

2. In the Tools tab, choose the Elliptical Marquee tool (Elliptical Marquee tool).

3. Place the pointer roughly in the middle of the bolt.

4. After clicking, start moving. Then, as you drag the selection to the outer border of the screw, hit Alt (Windows) or Option (MacOS) while holding down the mouse button.

5. Release the mouse button first, then release Alt or Option once you've chosen the complete screw head (and the Shift key if you used it). You'll use this selection in the following task, so don't deselect.

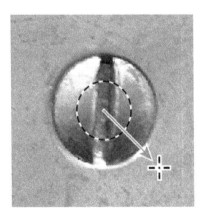

6. Use one of the earlier techniques to reposition the selection border if required. Select the screw once more if you unintentionally released the Alt or Option key before releasing the cursor button.

How to Resize the contents of a

selection

The screw must be moved first, but it is too big for the available area. So it needs to be resized as well.

1. Verify that the screw is still chosen before you start. Re-select it by completing the prior exercise if it isn't.

2. To make the full image fit within the document window, select View > Fit On Screen.

3. In the Tools tab, choose the Move tool (Move tool).

   Within the screw option, place the pointer.

4. Drag the screw onto the shadow box's bottom right area.

5. Select Scale under Modify > Transform. Around the pick, a bounding box appears.

6. To make the screw smaller so that it can rest on the shadow box frame, drag one of the corner points inward until the screw is about 40% of its initial size.

7. To finalize the modification and eliminate the transformation bounding box, press Enter or Return.

8. After adjusting the screw's size, use the Move tool to move it to the corner of the shadow box frame.

9. To save your work, pick File > Save while keeping the screw selected.

How to Crop an image

Once your composition is positioned, you will crop the picture to its final size. Use either the Crop tool or the Crop command to crop a picture.

1. To switch from the current tool to the Crop tool, select the Crop tool (Crop tool) or hit C. A crop boundary is shown around the complete image in Photoshop.

2. Ensure no ratio values are defined and that Ratio is chosen from the Preset pop-up menu in the options bar. Click Clean if there are any errors. Afterward, make sure Erase Cropped Pixels is chosen.

   You can easily crop the image to any proportions when a Ratio is chosen, but no ratio values are provided.

3. Drag the crop handles to remove the backgrounds from the original objects at the bottom of the picture and place the shadow box in the highlighted area. Trim the image so that a consistent white border surrounds it.

4. Click the Commit Current Crop Operation icon (located in the Crop tool's options bar) when you're happy with how the crop region is positioned.

5. Choose File > Save to save your work.

Chapter 4: Layer Basics

How to Use the Layers panel

The Layers panel displays thumbnails of the material on each layer and a list of all the layers that make up an image. The Layers panel allows you to conceal, examine, move, remove, rename, and merge layers. As you edit the layers, the layer thumbnails are immediately updated.

1. Select Window > Layers if the Layers panel is not displayed in the work area.

From top to bottom, the 04Working.psd File's Layers window displays the following five layers: Postage, HAWAII, Flower, Pineapple, and Background.

2. If the Background layer isn't already chosen, choose it to activate it. Take note of the Background layer's layer symbol and thumbnail:

- The layer is shielded from layer changes when the lock symbol (Lock icon (Layers panel)) is present. The choices above the layer list are, therefore, not accessible. For example, the layer substance can still be changed by painting on it.

- The eye symbol (Eye icon (Layers panel)) indicates the layer's visibility in the document window. The document window no longer shows that layer if you select the eye.

The postcard must first add a picture of the Beach as the first step in this endeavor. The beach pictures will first be opened in Photoshop.

3. Open the Beach.psd File in Photoshop by selecting File> Open, go to the subdirectory, and double-click it.

The Layers panel transforms to show the Beach's active layer information. PSD data. Take note that the Beach only displays one dimension. Picture in psd: Layer 1. It can use layer characteristics like transparency because it is not a Background layer.

How to Rearrange layers

The stacking sequence refers to the arrangement of layers within an image. The stacking order affects the image's perception; rearranging the layers can make specific portions of the image look ahead of or behind others.

The layers will be rearranged so that an image presently hidden in the File is in front of the beach image.

1. You can make each level visible by selecting the Show/Hide Visibility column next to the layer names for Postage, HAWAII, Flower, Pineapple, and Background.

Images on other layers have almost completely obscured the beach picture.

2. Drag the Beach layer up in the Layers panel in the middle of the Pineapple and Flower layers. As you drag, a blue line shows you where the layer will land.

The beach image shows under the postmark, flower, and "HAWAII," but on top of the pineapple and background images as the beach layer moves up one step in the stacking order.

How to change the opacity of a layer

Any layer's opacity can be decreased to make the levels beneath visible. The postmark on the blossom, in this instance, is too dark. You'll adjust the Postage layer's opacity to let the flower and other images shine through.

1. The Opacity tool will appear after selecting the Postage layer and clicking the arrow next to the Opacity field. To 25%, move the slider. You can also enter "25" or clear the Opacity label in the Opacity box.

It becomes partly transparent to see the layers beneath the Postage layer more clearly. Remember that the opacity shift impacts only the Postage layer's content. The HAWAII, Pineapple, Beach, and Flower sections are still opaque.

2. The Save option is found under File > Save.

How to Apply a gradient to a layer

A color gradient can cover all or a portion of a component. For example, in this illustration, you will use a gradient to make the word "HAWAII" more colorful. The gradient will be applied after you have chosen the characters.

1. To activate the HAWAII layer, select it in the Layers window.

2. Select Pixels by selecting the HAWAII layer image with the right-click or control-click menu.

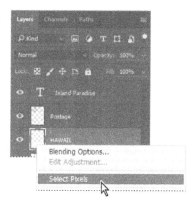

All opaque pixels are chosen on the HAWAII layer (the white writing). After choosing the area to fill, you will now add a gradient.

3. Tap on the Gradient tool can be found in the Tools menu.

4. Choose a vivid orange color in the Color Picker by clicking the Foreground Color swatch in the Tools window, then click OK. There should still be a clean background.

5. Make sure the Linear gradient is chosen in the Gradient tool's options bar by clicking the Linear Gradient button.

6. To access the Gradient Picker, pick the arrow next to the Gradient Editor box in the options bar. Click anywhere outside the Gradient Picker to dismiss it after selecting the Foreground To Background swatch (the first one in the Basics group).

7. Drag the Gradient tool from the bottom of the characters to the top while the selection is still active. Hold down the Shift key while dragging. If you want to, make sure you raise the object directly up. Release the mouse button once the pointer has reached the apex of the letters.

   The type is covered in a gradient that starts orange at the bottom and progressively transitions to white at the top.

8. Save the task you have already completed.

How to Apply a layer style

You can improve a layer by adding a shadow, stroke, satin sheen, or other unique effects from a selection of automatic and editable layer styles. These styles are simple to use and connect to the layer you choose.

Clicking the eye symbol in the Layers panel will enable you to hide layer styles like layers. Since layer patterns are non-destructive, you can change or eliminate them whenever you want.

You previously added a stroke to the beach picture using a layer style. You will now apply drop shadows to make the text stand out.

1. Select Layer > Layer Style > Drop Shadow should be selected after selecting the Island Paradise component.

2. Make sure the Preview checkbox is chosen in the Layer Style dialog box before moving the dialog box if required so that you can see the text "Island Paradise" in the image window. Now a falling shadow has been added.

3. Select Use Global Light in the Structure section, and then enter the following information:

   - Blend setting multiplies

   - Blend Mode: Multiply

   - Opacity: 75%

   - CD Angle: 78 degrees

   - Distance: 5 px

   - Spread: 30%

   - Size: 10 px

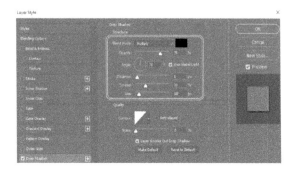

Many layer effects that use shading are possible with a global (shared) lighting angle when Use Global Light is selected. Every other effect with Use Global Light selected inherits the lighting angle you specify in one of these effects.

4. Click OK to confirm the settings and dismiss the Layer Style dialog box.

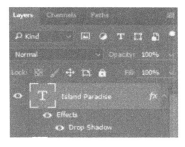

5. Ensure that both objects nested in the Island Paradise layer have eye icons.

6. Press Alt (Windows) or Option (Mac) and move the Effects listing or the fx symbol (Layers panel: Effects symbol) for the Island Paradise layer onto the HAWAII layer in the Layers panel.

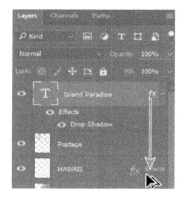

The HAWAII layer has the Drop Shadow layer style applied, with the parameters from the Island Paradise layer being copied over. In addition, the phrase "HAWAII" will now have a green stroke added to it.

7. Click the Add A Layer Style button (Effects symbol (Layers panel)) at the panel's bottom, select the HAWAII layer, and then select stroke from the pop-up selection.

8. Enter the following options in the Layer Style dialog box's Structure area:

   • Size: 4 px

   • Position: Outside

   • Blend Mode: Normal

   • Opacity: 100%

   • Color: Green

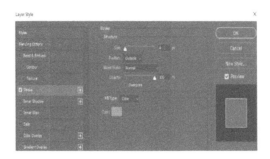

9. Click OK to put the motion into action.

10. After choosing the Flower component, pick layer> Layer Style > Drop Shadow. Then, change the following settings in the Organization section:

- Opacity: 60%

- Distance: 13 px

- Spread: 9%

- Ensure Multiply is the Blend Option and Use Global Light is checked.

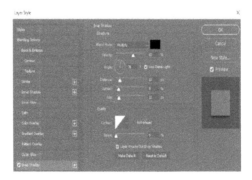

11. While the Layer Style dialog box is still visible, click the word "Satin" on the left to pick it and display its options. Use these options after making sure Invert is selected:

- Color: Choose a color that brings out the blossom's color (next to Blend Mode), like a fuchsia hue.

- Opacity: 20%

- Distance: 22 px

The satin layer effect employs interior shading to create a satiny finish. The contour determines the shape of the impact, and Invert flips the contour curve.

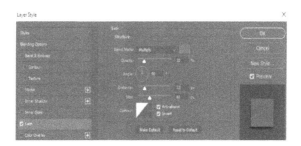

12. Click OK to apply both layer styles. The Layers window displays the two-layer styles for the Flower layer. The Flower layer's look with and without the layer styles can be contrasted using the eye icons.

How to Add an adjustment layer

You can use adjustment layers to modify colors and tones without permanently changing the image's pixel values. You can experiment with different colors frequently because, for example, the change only affects the adjustment layer when you add a Color Balance adjustment layer to an image. You can hide or remove the correction layer if you return to the original pixel values.

Apply a Hue/Saturation adjustment layer to the purple flower in this photo to change its color and saturation. An adjustment layer affects all layers below it in the image's stacking order unless a selection is active when you make it or you create a clipping mask.

1. Select the Flower2 layer in the Layers pane.

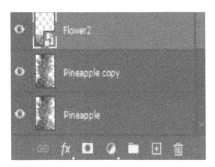

2. Click the Hue/Saturation icon in the Adjustments box to add a Hue/Saturation adjustment layer.

3. Make the subsequent modifications to the Properties panel:

- Hue: 43

- Saturation: 19

- Lightness: 0

The modifications affect the backdrop, clouds, pineapple copy, flower2, and pineapple layers. Despite the interesting outcome, you only want to change the Flower2 layer.

4. The Properties panel's Create Clipping Mask icon should be clicked (or the Create Clipping Mask option in the Layers panel). You can see it as the first button along the bottom of the panel when the Properties panel displays choices for a layer that can serve as a clipping mask, like an adjustment layer.

The correction layer impacts only the Flower2 layer.

How to Update layer effects

Layer effects are instantly updated whenever you modify a layer. As you alter the text, the layer impact will be updated.

1. Pick the Island Paradise layer in the Layers pane.

2. From the Options menu, select the Horizontal Type tool (Horizontal Type tool).

3. Hit Enter or Return after slightly modifying the Size setting in the options section.

4. Move the "Island Paradise" style layer as required using the Move tool.

5. Choose File > Save.

How to Create a border from a selection

The postcard from Honolulu is almost finished. Nearly every element in the composition is placed properly. Your final touches will be positioning the postmark and adding a white envelope border.

1. Ensure Auto-Select is off in the options menu and choose the Move tool.

2. Using the Move tool (Move tool), select the Postage layer, and then move it to the image's center-right, as shown in the example.

3. Click the New Layer option (Layers panel) at the bottom after selecting the Island Paradise layer in the Layers panel.

4. Pick All from the menu.

5. Tap Select > Modify > Border. Enter 10 pixels in the Width field of the Border Selection dialog window, then click OK.

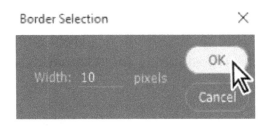

6. Select Foreground Color from the Contents menu in the Fill dialog window, then click OK.

7. Pick instead of Deselect.

8. Rename the layer Border by clicking twice on Layer 1's name in the Layers window.

How to Flatten and Save files

After altering your image's layers, you can combine or flatten the layers to shrink the file size. All the elements are combined into a single background layer after flattening. However, layers cannot be edited after they have been flattened, so you should wait to flatten an image until you are happy with all of your design choices. It's a good idea to save a copy of your initial PSD files with all of their layers intact rather than flattening them in case you need to edit a layer.

Look at the two figures for the file size in the status bar at the bottom of the document window to understand what flattening does. The first figure shows the file size of a flattened version of the image. The second figure indicates the size of the File without flattening. For example, if compressed, this lesson's File would be between 2 and 3 MB, but it is much bigger. Flattening thus makes sense in this situation.

1. If you're not in text-editing mode, choose any tool other than the Type tool (Horizontal Type tool). To ensure that all of your modifications have been saved in the File, select File> Save (if it is an option).

2. Copy from the Image menu.

3. Name the File 04Flat.psd in the Duplicate Image dialog window, then click OK.

4. Close the 04Working.psd File but keep the 04Flat.psd File active.

5. From the Layers panel option, select Flatten Image.

6. Select Edit > Save. The Save As dialog box shows even though you selected Save rather than Save As because this document still needs to be saved to storage.

7. Once you have confirmed that the location is in your computer's folder, select Save to accept the default settings and save the flattened File.

You have saved two copies of the File: the original with all the layers intact and a one-layer, flattened duplicate.

Chapter 5: Quick Fixes

Getting started

Not every picture needs to be complicatedly altered using Photoshop's advanced features. In reality, you can frequently quickly improve an image once you are familiar with Photoshop. Knowing what is feasible and where to look for what you need is the key.

You can combine or use these techniques separately if an image requires more assistance.

1. Launch Photoshop.

Hold down Ctrl+Alt+Shift (Windows) or Command+Option+Shift (macOS) to return to the preset settings.

2. To delete the Adobe Photoshop Settings file, respond "Yes" to the offer.

How to improve a snapshot

A photo may not need to appear professional if you share it with relatives and friends. However, glowing eyes are different from what you want, and it would be preferable if the image were light enough to reveal crucial details. You can quickly edit a picture using the tools in Photoshop.

How to correct red eye

The red eye happens when the camera light reflects off a subject's retina. Because the subject's irises are wide open, it frequently happens in pictures shot in a dark room. Luckily, red eyes in Photoshop are simple to remove. In this practice, you will remove the red eye from the portrait's subject's eyes.

1. To launch Adobe Bridge, select File> Browse In Bridge.

2. Click the Lessons folder in Bridge's Favorites menu. Double-click the folder to launch it after that in the Content window.

3. If required, adjust the thumbnail slider to get a clear view of the thumbnail previews. View the RedEye Start.jpg and RedEye End.psd folders after that.

   The red eye can detract from the image's main topic and make an ordinary person or animal seem out of the ordinary. However, red eyes are simple to fix in Photoshop, and you can easily brighten this picture.

4. To launch Photoshop, double-click the RedEye Start.jpg image.

5. Select File> Save As, enter RedEye Working.psd as the file name, select Photoshop as the Format, and press Save.

6. Select the Zoom tool (Zoom tool) to see the baby's irises, then drag to zoom in. If Scrubby Zoom isn't chosen, you can zoom in by dragging an outline around the eyes.

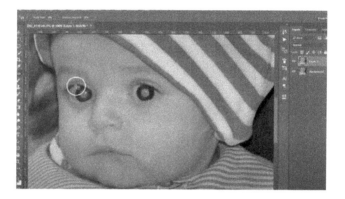

7. Under the Spot Healing Brush tool, select the Red Eye (Red-Eye tool).

8. Reduce the Pupil Size to 23% and the Darken Amount to 62% in the options menu.

How black the pupil should be is determined by the Darken Amount.

9. Click the baby's left eye iris. The reflection in crimson vanishes.

The baby's right eye's pupil can also be clicked to eliminate the crimson reflection there.

10. Save your work and view the full image by selecting View > Fit On Screen.

How to Adjust facial features with liquify

The Liquify filter is handy when you want to distort just a portion of a picture. It has Face-Aware Liquify options that can identify faces in images automatically and then let you quickly change facial features like the size or separation of the eyes. It is helpful for photographs used in fashion and advertising when capturing a specific expression or look rather than accurately capturing a specific person.

1. Continue to open RedEye Working.psd and select Filter > Liquify.

2. Click the right-facing triangle in the Properties window to expand the Face-Aware Liquify options if they are collapsed (hidden).

3. Ensure the Eyes section is expanded, and Eye Size and Eye Height should be set to the link symbol (Liquify Link Icon). Select 10 for the eye height and 32 for the eye size.

You can set separate values for the left and right eyes when the link icon (Liquify Link Icon) is not chosen for an Eyes option.

4. Enter 5 for Smile and 9 for Mouth Height after expanding the Mouth area.

5. Enter 40 for the jawline and 50 for the face width after ensuring the Face Shape area is expanded.

6. To see how your changes affected the picture before and after, deselect and then reselect the Preview option.

To better understand the potential for quick, simple changes, feel free to play around with any of the Face-Aware Liquify choices.

7. For Liquify to end, click OK. Once your modifications are saved, close the document.

How to Blur around a subject

Bridge's start and finish files should be your first port of call.

1. To launch Adobe Bridge, select File> Browse In Bridge.

2. Click the Lessons folder in Bridge's Favorites menu. Double-click the folder to launch it after that in the Content window.

3. Examine the thumbnail samples of Egret Start.jpg and Egret End.psd side by side.

4. Select File> Open As Smart Object and File > Back To Adobe Photoshop, respectively.

5. Click OK or Open after choosing the Egret Start.jpg image from the folder.

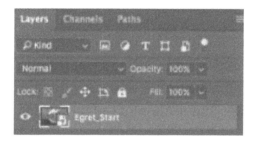

6. Click Save after selecting File> Save As, giving the image the name Egret Working.psd, and selecting Photoshop as the Format. In the dialog window for Photoshop Format Options, click OK.

7. Select Iris Blur under Filter > Blur Collection. The dialog window for Blur Gallery appears.

   A blur ellipse surrounds your picture. By adjusting the center pin, feather handles, and ellipse handles, you can change the position and range of the blur. There are also expandable field Blur, Tilt-Shift Blur, Path Blur, and

Spin Blur panels in the top-right corner of the Blur Gallery task space; these are additional kinds of blur you can use.

8. Drag the central pin down until it is at the bird's base.

9. Click the ellipse and drag inward to concentrate more closely on the bird.

10. As you click and drag the feather handles to resemble those in the first picture below, hold down the Alt (Windows) or Option (MacOS) key. You can move each handle independently by pressing Alt or Option.

11. Lower the blur to 5 px by clicking and dragging the Blur ring to gradually but noticeably blur the image. You can also alter the same value by adjusting the Blur slider in the Iris Blur section of the Blur Tools panel.

12. To use the blur, click OK in the options window.

There might be too little distortion. The blur will be edited to increase it marginally.

13. Double-click the Egret layer in the Layers window to reopen the Blur Gallery. To make the change, change the blur to 6 px and click OK in the options bar.

14. Close the document after saving it.

How to Create a panorama

A view may occasionally be too expansive for one picture. Creating panoramas in Photoshop is simple so viewers can see the complete impact.

Once more, you'll glance at the final File to determine your course of action.

1. Select "File" > "Explore In Bridge."

2. If you haven't already, go to the section. View the Skyline End.psd thumbnail sample after that.

To give viewers a feeling of the entire scene, you'll stitch together four images of the Seattle skyline into a single wide panorama picture. Creating a panorama only takes a few clicks to stitch together numerous images. Photoshop handles the remainder.

3. Go back to Photoshop.

4. Select File> Automate > Photomerge in Photoshop without any images open.

5. Click Browse in the Source Files section, then go to the Files For Panorama subdirectory.

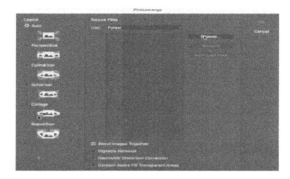

6. Click OK or Open after selecting every picture in the folder with the Shift key.

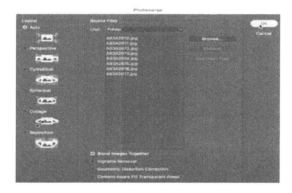

7. Select Perspective in the Photomerge text box's Layout section.

8. Choose Blend Photos Together, Vignette Removal, Geometric Distortion Correction, and Content Aware Fill Transparent Areas from the options at the bottom of the Photomerge dialog window. Then press OK.

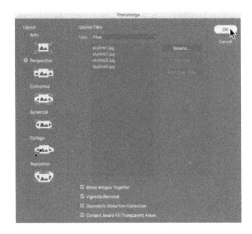

Merge Pictures Instead of producing a straightforward rectangular merge, Together blends pictures based on the best possible borders between them. When merging pictures with darker edges, vignette removal helps guarantee uniform brightness. Barrell, pincushion, or fish-eye distortion are all addressed by geometric distortion correction. The empty spaces between the merged picture's edges and the canvas's sides are instantly filled with content using Content Aware Fill Transparent Areas.

How to Fill empty areas when cropping

With two exceptions, the panorama image is excellent. The horizon is slightly off-center, and the lower handrail is missing where the rocks on the right slope into the water. If the image were rotated, empty spaces might appear at the corners, necessitating a closer crop and resulting in the loss of some of the image. Fortunately, straightening and cropping can also leave empty spaces that can be filled in by Content-Aware technology. This technology also filled in empty spaces left by the panorama merge.

1. Make sure Photoshop is open, and in the Layers panel, pick the Background layer.

2. Select Flatten Picture under Layer.

3. Choose the Crop tool from the Tools menu.

The crop rectangle and its handles surround the picture.

4. Ensure Content-Aware is chosen when you choose the Straighten icon (Straighten icon) in the options bar.

5. Place the Straighten pointer on the horizon at the left edge of the image, and then drag it to the right to create a Straighten line parallel to the horizon. When you reach the right edge of the image, where the horizon ends, release the mouse button.

6. Drag the picture down until the incomplete portion of the lower guardrail is outside the crop rectangle while the crop rectangle is still active.

7. To implement the current crop settings, click the Commit (check mark) button in the options bar. Content-Aware, The top and sides of the picture are filled in by cropping.

8. Close the document after saving your modifications.

How to Correct image distortion

The Lens Correction filter corrects typical camera lens flaws like chromatic aberration, vignetting, and barrel and pincushion distortion. Straight lines bow out toward the edges of the picture due to barrel distortion, a flaw in the lens. The opposite impact, known as pincushion distortion, causes straight lines to curve inward. A colored fringe can be seen around the margins of image objects due to chromatic aberration. When an image's borders, mainly its corners, are darker than its center, vignetting is the result.

Some lenses have these flaws depending on the f-stop or focal range. The Lens Correction filter can apply settings depending on the camera, lens, and focal length used to create the picture. The filter can also rotate a picture or correct perspective issues brought on by vertical or horizontal camera tilt. Making these changes using the grid of the filter is simpler and more precise than doing so with the Transform command.

1. Select "File" > "Browse In Bridge."

2. If you haven't already, go to the folder and check out the samples.

3. To launch Photoshop, double-click the file.

4. Select Save As under Media. Columns Working.psd should be saved in the folder with the name you gave it in the Save As dialog window. If the Photoshop Format Options dialog window shows up, click OK.

5. Select Lens Adjustment under Filter. The dialog window for lens correction appears.

6. Ensure Show Grid and Preview are checked at the bottom of the dialog window.

7. Ensure Transparency is chosen from the Edge option and Auto Scale Image is selected in the Correction section of the Autocorrect tab.

8. Choose the Custom option.

9. To remove the barrel distortion in the picture, move the Remove Distortion slider to about +52.00 on the Custom tab. Alternatively, you can choose the Remove Distortion tool and drag in the picture preview area until the columns are straight. The picture borders bow inward as a result of the adjustment. The Lens Correction filter, however, automatically scales the picture to correct the borders because you chose Auto Scale Image.

10. Click OK to save your modifications and close the Lens Correction dialog window.

The low shooting position lessens the wide-angle lens's curving distortion.

11. (Optional) Press Ctrl+Alt+Z (Windows) or Command+Option+Z (macOS) to undo the filter, then hit the same keys to apply it again to compare the image before and after the most recent change. You can frequently hit that key to switch between the last two states of the document because it is the keyboard shortcut for the Edit > Toggle Last State command.

12. If the Photoshop Format Options dialog box appears, select File> Save to save your changes, then click OK to close the picture.

How to Extend depth of field

The depth of field, or the range of lengths in focus, can be limited in some situations, forcing you to decide whether to concentrate on a scene's foreground or background. For example, take a series of photographs focused along the distances you want to appear sharp if you want a broader range of distances to be in focus (more depth of field). Still, it isn't feasible due to equipment or location restrictions. So instead, the images can be combined using a technique known as focus stacking in Photoshop. With the combined depth of field of the image collection, you obtain a single image.

Use a tripod to keep the camera steady because you'll need to align the pictures precisely. However, you can get excellent results if you can frame and align them consistently with a handheld camera. In this practice, you'll be enhancing an image of a wine glass in front of a beach by adding depth of field.

1. Select "File" > "Explore In Bridge."

2. To view the Glass Start.psd file, double-click it.

3. Select Save As under File. Save the document as Glass Working.psd in the subdirectory. If the Photoshop Format Options dialog window shows up, click OK.

4. Hide the Beach layer in the Layers window to make the Glass layer the only one that is visible. The backdrop is blurry but the glass is sharp. Then reveal the Beach layer once more. The shoreline is now sharp, but the glass is hazy.

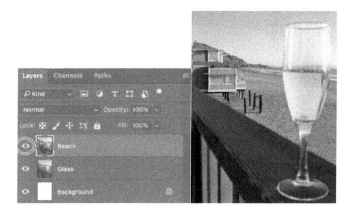

5. Shift-click to pick both layers in the Layers panel.

6. Select Auto-Align Layers under Edit.

7. If it still needs to be chosen, choose Auto. Make sure neither Geometric Distortion nor Vignette Reduction is chosen. To align the layers, select OK after that.

8. You can now blend the layers since they are precisely aligned.

9. Ensure the Layers panel's selection of both levels is still active. Select Modify > Auto-Blend Layers after that.

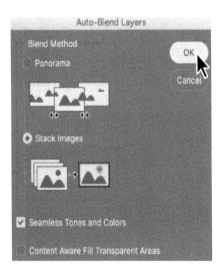

10. If they still need to be chosen, choose Seamless Tones And Colors and Stack Images. Click OK after making sure Content Aware Fill Transparent Areas is not chosen.

    Because Auto-Blend Layers combine the sharpest portions of each picture, the wine glass and the shoreline behind it are both in sharp focus. Observe in the Layers panel that both initial layers have been kept and that the blending was accomplished using masks that concealed the areas of each picture that were out of focus, leaving only the sharp portions of each image visible.

11. Save your work, then close the File.

How to Remove objects using Content-Aware Fill

Instead of leaving a blank space, you'll use Content-Aware Fill to remove an unwanted item and have Photoshop convincingly fill the area.

1. Select "File" > "Explore In Bridge."

2. To launch Photoshop, double-click the JapaneseGarden Start.jpg image.

3. Select Photoshop as the document type, give the new File the name JapaneseGarden Working.psd, and then select File> Save As. Press Save. If the Photoshop Format Options dialog window shows up, click OK.

4. Choose the Lasso tool (Lasso tool).

5. Drag a selection marquee to encompass the rock on the left, its reflection below it, and a portion of the surrounding ocean. The choice may be roughly made.

6. Select Content-Aware Fill under Modify.

7. When the options bar shows that the brush size is approximately 175 pixels, press the [key to scale down the sampling brush tool. The usual selection when you launch the Content-Aware Fill dialog box is the Sampling Brush tool.

8. To exclude it from the sampling area, paint over undesirable areas (such as vegetation or the edge where the vegetation joins the water). You can no longer see the green sampling hue in the excluded areas. The fill is changed as you proceed, and the updated outcomes can be assessed in the Preview panel.

9. You can cease painting as soon as the fill appears to be made up only of water and realistic reflections.

10. Click Apply if there are any extra fields you want to fill in. You can now make a new selection to fill since the prior selection has been committed.

11. When done, select Select > Deselect by clicking OK.

12. After saving your work, exit the window.

Chapter 6: Masks and Channels

Working with masks and channels

A digital picture is an opaque rectangle when it leaves the camera. Therefore, you conceal the region outside the topic to combine it with other image parts. Alternatively, you can only use a filter or modification layer on a portion of a layer. Using a mask, a tool for designating layer regions as transparent is the suggested method for accomplishing both.

Because a mask can be reversed, it is more helpful than deleting unwanted portions of a layer: A mask, for instance, enables you to restore the trimmed area to fix a mistake where you unintentionally cut off part of the topic.

Getting started

You will first examine the image you will produce using channels and masks.

1. Start Photoshop and press Ctrl+Alt+Shift (Windows) or Command+Option+Shift (Mac) to return to the preset settings.

2. To delete the Adobe Photoshop Settings file, respond "Yes" to the offer.

3. To launch Adobe Bridge, select File> Browse In Bridge.

4. On the Bridge window's left side, select the Favorites option. Double-click the folder in the Content window after selecting the Lessons folder.

5. Examine the 06End.psd document. Slide the thumbnail slider to the right to enlarge it to see it more clearly. It is located at the bottom of the Bridge window.

6. To view 06Start.psd in Photoshop, double-click the thumbnail. If an Embedded Profile Mismatch dialog window appears, click OK.

7. Change the File's name to 06Working.psd by selecting File> Save As, then hit Save. If the Photoshop Format Options dialog window shows up, click OK.

How to Use Select And Mask and Select Subject

A task space called Select And Mask in Photoshop contains tools dedicated to building and perfecting masks. First, use the Select Subject in Select And Mask to quickly create the mask, isolating the model from the backdrop. Then, you will improve the mask using additional Select and Mask tools, like the Quick Selection tool.

1. Ensure both layers are displayed, and the Model layer is selected in the Layers panel.

2. Select > Select And Cover is the choice.

3. The Overlay can be selected by clicking the View option in the Properties panel's View Mode section. Instead of the onion skin checkerboard pattern, the masked region is now displayed as a semitransparent red hue. Because nothing has been covered yet, it is stable.

4. Choose Subject by clicking the button in the options column.

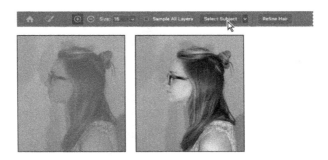

5. Black & White can be selected by clicking the View option in the Properties panel's View Mode section. The mask edge is easier to see with the aid of this View Mode.

6. Expand the Refine Mode if necessary in the Properties window, then select Color Aware. Click OK if a notification pops up. The mask's border is altered.

   Potential topic edges are interpreted differently by the two refined modes. On straightforward backgrounds, Color Aware can be effective. However, object Aware may function better on more complex backgrounds.

Select Edit > Toggle Last State to switch between the two results if you want to compare them.

7. Choose Overlay from the View menu in the Properties panel's View Mode section to compare the edge more effectively to the image.

8. Be sure to select the Quick Selection tool (Quick Selection tool). Set up a brush with a 15 px size in the options bar.

9. To include the missed areas in the selection, drag the Quick Selection tool over them (without going into the background). You don't need to be precise because the Quick Selection tool fills in the selection as it locates content edges. You can drag more than once after releasing the mouse button.

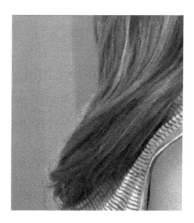

10. Select On Layers from the View menu by clicking it again in the View Mode section. It demonstrates how any layers behind this layer will appear when the current

Select and Mask settings are applied. In this instance, you are watching a preview of how the Model layer will be masked over the Episode Background layer under the current settings.

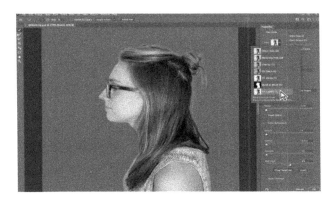

How to Manipulate an image with Puppet Warp

Your ability to manipulate an image is flexible with the Puppet Warp function. Similar to manipulating the strings on a puppet, you can move things like hair or a limb. Wherever you want to restrict mobility, place pins. The model's head will be tilted back using Puppet Warp so that she looks to be looking upward.

1. To see the complete model, zoom out.

2. Select Edit > Puppet Warp while the Model Copy layer is active in the Layers window.

3. In this instance, a mesh forms over the model and covers the visible portions of the layer. Pins will be inserted into

the mesh where you want to regulate movement (or ensure no movement).

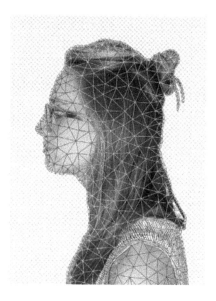

4. Click to add pins to the torso and the base of the head. Clicking causes Puppet Warp to place a pin each time. Pins between 10 and 12 should function.

5. At the nape of the neck, choose the fastener. The middle of the pin displays a blue dot to show that it has been chosen.

6. Select Option (Windows) or Alt (Mac) (macOS). A larger circular surrounds the pin, and a double curved arrow is displayed next to it. As you drag the pointer to rotate the head backward, keep pressing Alt or Option. The options bar displays the rotation angle; to rotate the head back, enter 170 there.

7. When you are happy with the rotation, press Enter or Return or click the Commit Puppet Warp button (Commit button) in the options bar.

8. Save your current work.

How to use an alpha channel to create a shadow

Channels enable you to access particular types of information, just as various types of information are stored on different layers in an image. For example, grayscale pictures are stored for selections in alpha channels. For example, red, green, blue, and composite channels are naturally present in an RGB image, and they store information about each color.

To distinguish between channels and layers, consider that a picture's color and selection information is contained in a channel. In contrast, painting, shapes, text, and other content are contained in a layer.

The transparent regions of the Model copy layer will first be turned into a selection, which will then be filled with Black on another layer to produce a shadow. You'll now save the selection in its current state as an alpha channel so that you can load it again later if necessary because the selection will be changed to create the shadow.

1. Ctrl-click (Windows) or Command-click (Mac OS) the layer thumbnail icon for the Model Copy layer in the Layers window. Select the masked region.

2. Pick > Save Selection is the option. Ensure New is selected from the Channel menu in the Save Selection dialog window.

Next, give the channel the name Model Sketch and press OK.

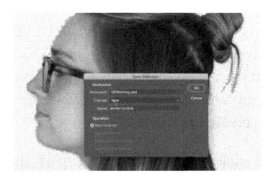

3. Neither the text window nor the Layers panel is altered. But the Channels section now includes a brand-new channel called Model Outline. The option is still open.

4. Select > Select And Mask while the Shadow layer is chosen. The current pick is then loaded into the Select and Mask task space.

5. Choose On Black from the View option in the Properties panel's View Mode section.

6. Change the Shift Edge slider in the Global Refinements area to +36%.

7. Make sure the selection is chosen in the Output To menu in the Output Settings section, and then press OK.

8. Select Fill > Modify. Select Black from the Contents menu in the Fill dialog window, then click OK.

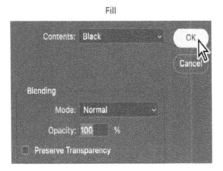

9. Set the layer opacity to 30% in the Layers window.

10. To delete the selection, pick Select > Deselect.

11. Select Rotate under Modify > Transform. You can manually rotate the shadow or input a 15-degree angle in the Rotate field of the options bar. Then either type 545 in the X field of the options bar or drag the shadow to the left. To accept the transformation, hit Enter or Return or click the Commit button (Commit button) in the options bar.

12. Make the Episode Background layer visible by clicking the eye symbol, then remove the Model layer (the one without the mask).

13. To save your current work, select Edit > Save.

How to create a pattern for the background

The background of the episode graphic's style features a pattern. The pattern can be rapidly made by modifying a vector graphic shape.

How to customize a polygon shape

Star shapes are the basis for the backdrop. Unfortunately, Photoshop doesn't have a star tool, but you can make one by modifying a shape with the Polygon tool.

1. Open the 06Pattern.psd File located in the subdirectory. It launches in a separate text tab.

2. Choose the Polygon tool paired with the Rectangle tool (Polygon tool icon).

Make sure the tool is set to Shape in the options menu.

3. Draw a polygon shape about 340 pixels broad while holding down Shift. After drawing, you can use the Move tool to move it if it isn't exactly in the middle of the canvas.

4. Set the Fill to None, the Stroke to 20px, and a blue Stroke color a little darker than the background (we used R=27, G=58, B=185) while keeping the shape layer selected in the Properties window.

5. Make the star ratio 70% and the polygon's number of sides 8. The number of sides changes to the number of points when the star ratio falls below 100%.

6. Drag and drop the star-shaped layer onto the Create A New Layer button in the Layers panel to replicate it.

7. Set the Rotate angle to 24 in the Properties tab.

8. Select Edit > Free Transform Path, then drag a corner handle to reduce the size of the duplicate star layer so that it fits inside the bigger star while holding down the Alt (Windows) or Option (MacOS) key. To implement the change, press Enter or Return.

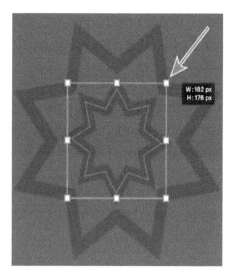

9. To examine the design as a pattern, select view> Pattern Preview. Click OK if a notification pops up. Only the canvas's original shape is editable, but Pattern Preview adjusts to consider your changes.

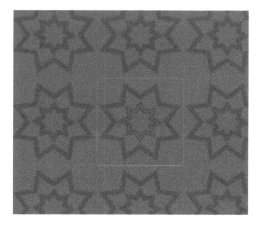

10. Look for a tiny circular handle inside the top-right star point of Polygon 1 (the large star) when using the Move tool and the Layers panel's Polygon 1 selection. Make

sure Show Transform Controls is selected in the options menu and raise the view magnification if you still can't see the handle.

11. Drag the handle to convert the pointed star points to rounder star points. A radius of 20 squares was employed. The sample design is updated.

12. Choose Polygon 1 duplicate from the Layers panel (the small star). Set the Number Of Points to 15 and the Stroke Width to 15 px in the Properties window.

13. Select Podcast Pattern from the Edit > Define Pattern menu, then select OK. You can use the resulting pattern preset in any Photoshop project.

14. Change the File's name to 06Pattern Working.psd by selecting File> Save As, then hit Save. If the Photoshop Format Options dialog window shows up, click OK.

15. Select the Episode Backdrop layer in 06Working.psd after switching.

16. Select the pattern from the Create New Fill Or Adjustment Layer drop-down menu in the Layers window.

17. Select the blue pattern you made at the bottom of the list by clicking the pattern picker in the Pattern Fill dialog window. Click OK after setting the Scale to 35% and the Tilt to 45 degrees.

18. Save your progress.